MAKING

MW01119005

BATH BOMBS FOR

BEGINNERS

Profitable Techniques, Recipes, And

Guidelines For Novices: Essential Oil

Blends, Natural Ingredients, Packaging

Tips, And Profitable Marketing

Strategies

DAYANA JIMENA

CONTENTS

DISCLAIMER

This book, is intended to provide educational and informational content about the process of production, marketing and distribution. The author and publisher have made every effort to ensure the accuracy of the information presented herein. However, the information provided in this book is based on the author's research, experience, and knowledge.

It is important to note that the author does not endorse, promote, or have any affiliations with specific individuals, products, websites, organizations, or other entities that may be mentioned in this book.

Any references to such entities are purely for informational purposes and should not be construed as endorsements.

Readers are encouraged to conduct their own research, seek professional advice, and exercise their own judgment when implementing the techniques, strategies, or suggestions outlined in this book. The author and publisher disclaim any liability for any loss or damage caused directly or indirectly by the information provided in this book.

By reading this book, the reader acknowledges and agrees to the terms of this disclaimer. If the reader does not agree with these terms, they should not use the information provided in this book.

ABOUT THIS BOOK

"Making and Selling Bath Bombs for Beginners" is an essential resource for those who are just beginning to explore the lucrative realm of bath bomb manufacturing and distribution. This exhaustive publication has been carefully curated to furnish novices with the fundamental understanding and abilities required to thrive in this fiercely competitive industry.

A comprehensive preface to this book furnishes an outline of the bath bomb sector and establishes the context for the information that follows. "Getting Started" offers readers a comprehensive guide to the preliminary stages of initiating their bath bomb-making endeavor, including the acquisition of essential materials and the establishment of a secure and conducive work environment.

This books "Ingredients and Supplies" provides an in-depth analysis of the essential components required in the production of bath bombs, emphasizing the significance of high-quality ingredients in attaining favorable outcomes for readers. The "Basic Bath Bomb Recipe" functions as a fundamental guide for novices, providing a straightforward yet impactful formula to initiate their formulations.

Individuals aspiring to create bath bombs will find valuable the chapters devoted to refining their creations by "Molding and Shaping Techniques" and "Adding Colors and Scents." Additionally, this book discusses essential elements including the "Drying and Curing Process" and "Packaging and Presentation," underscoring the importance of appealing to customers through aesthetics.

The guidance provided on "Marketing Your Bath Bombs," which encompasses tactics for both offline and online sales channels, is of equal importance. Through the examination of various strategies such as "Selling Online" and "Selling at Local Markets and Events," readers are provided with valuable knowledge regarding efficient communication with their intended audience while also addressing potential obstacles that may emerge.

By placing a strong emphasis on expansion and long-term viability, this book delves into the topics of "Scaling Up Your Business" and cultivating "Feedback and Customer Satisfaction." Additionally, it offers invaluable guidance on legal implications, sustainable methodologies, and the establishment of a unique brand image.

Throughout the expedition, readers are motivated to give utmost importance to safety measures, uphold scrupulous documentation practices, and consistently introduce novel product concepts. In addition to inventory administration and troubleshooting common issues, each element of establishing a prosperous bath bomb enterprise is thoroughly examined.

Fundamentally, "Making and Selling Bath Bombs for Beginners" functions as an all-encompassing guidebook that enables individuals with entrepreneurial aspirations to transform their fervor for bath bomb creation into a prosperous commercial enterprise.

CHAPTER ONE

Introduction

As an indulgence that provides a luxurious and calming experience in the convenience of one's own Jacuzzi, bath salts have gained widespread popularity.

By introducing color, fragrance, and moisturizing substances into the bathwater, these carbonated, aromatic cylinders elevate an ordinary relaxation to a sensory delight. It is a thrilling opportunity to investigate self-care, entrepreneurship, and creativity for individuals who are new to the tub bomb manufacturing and retailing industry.

Commencing Our Work

Before beginning production, it is critical to conduct an extensive investigation on bath bomb manufacturing.

This encompasses acquiring knowledge of the various ingredients, becoming acquainted with distinct recipes and techniques, and becoming acquainted with safety precautions. In addition, market demand, competition, and the intended market are factors that should influence your business strategy.

Invest in high-quality instruments and ingredients to ensure that you have everything required to produce successful bath bombs.

Molds, measuring utensils, mixing containers, and ingredients such as baking soda, citric acid, Epsom salt, and essential oils may be included. Establish a designated area with adequate storage and ventilation to facilitate the manufacturing process.

Components And Equipment

It is essential to comprehend the function of each component when formulating bath bubbles that are both effective and aesthetically pleasing. The fundamental elements comprise:

1. Baking Soda (Sodium Bicarbonate) aids in skin softening and induces a fizzy sensation.

2. Baking soda and citric acid react to produce the fizzing effect.

3. Epsom salt imparts a silky feel and aids in muscle relaxation.

4. Carrier oils offer hydration and nourishment to the epidermis, including almond oil, coconut oil, and grapeseed oil.

5. Essential oils offer both therapeutic and aromatic properties.

6. A binder, such as water or witch hazel, is utilized to secure the constituents.

When creating bath bombs, ensure that you are using premium ingredients to ensure their safety and efficacy. Consider purchasing supplies in volume to ensure product consistency and reduce expenses.

Routine Bath Bomb Formula

A rudimentary bath bomb formula can function as a cornerstone for innovation and personalization. Begin with the following fundamental recipe:

1 cup of baking powder

1/2 cup acidic (citric)

• One-half cup Epsom salt

• One-half cup cornstarch

• Two to three tablespoons of the carrier oil

• One to two teaspoons of witch hazel or water

(10-20 droplets) of essential oils

Coloring compounds, including natural pigments or mica particles, are discretionary.

1. Combine the dry ingredients (baking soda, citric acid, Epsom salt, and cornstarch) in a large mixing basin and stir thoroughly.

2. Combine the coloring agents, carrier oil, and water or witch hazel in a separate small basin.

3. While continuously whisking, gradually incorporate the liquid ingredients into the dry mixture until it forms a cohesive consistency when pressed with your palm. Excessive liquid addition should be avoided, as it may result in untimely fizzing.

4. When the mixture reaches the intended consistency, thoroughly compact it by packing it into bath bomb molds.

5. After allowing the bath bombs to solidify and dry in the molds for 24 to 48 hours, remove them with care.

6. Until ready to use or sell, store the bath bubbles in a secure container away from moisture and humidity.

By experimenting with various essential oil mixtures, colors, and supplementary components such as dried botanicals or flower petals, one can generate distinctive variations of this foundational bath bomb formula.

Imparting Scents And Colors

The incorporation of fragrances and colors into bath bombs permits artistic expression and enhances the sensory experience. Opt for pigments that are safe for the skin when choosing coloring agents, such as food coloring, cosmetic-grade colorants, or natural mica granules. Begin with a small quantity and increase it progressively until the desired hue is achieved.

Likewise, essential oils provide an extensive variety of aromatic alternatives, each possessing unique therapeutic advantages. Lavender is frequently used to induce relaxation, peppermint to stimulate, and citrus fragrances to impart a revitalizing aroma. Explore various oil combinations to develop distinctive fragrances for your bath bombs.

When incorporating fragrances and colors into the bath bomb formulation, exercise caution regarding possible skin sensitivities and allergies. In addition, it is critical to ensure transparency and inform customers by including a list of ingredients on the appropriate label of your products.

Through the acquisition of proficiency in these principles and methodologies, novices may commence a gratifying expedition into the production and commercialization of bath bombs, providing patrons with opulent bathing encounters while fostering their enterprising inclination.

Sure, let's examine each of these concepts regarding the production and sale of bath bubbles designed for novices:

CHAPTER TWO

Methods For Shaping And Molding

1. Spheres, hearts, or stars are examples of basic mold shapes that may be optimal for beginning crafters. These bath bomb shapes are versatile and yield aesthetically pleasing objects.

2. Silicone Molds: Bath bomb manufacturers favor silicone molds because of their adaptability and simplicity of use. They are available in a variety of sizes and configurations, which encourages design innovation.

3. Although bath bubbles can be manufactured consistently using molds, hand shaping can impart a sense of individuality. By applying pressure, rolling, or sculpting, one can generate textures and patterns of interest.

4. Layering and Embedding: To enhance the aesthetic allure of your bath bombs, experiment with layering various colored formulations or embedding tiny decorations such as flower petals or sparkles.

5. Consider developing expertise in the construction of custom molds through the utilization of materials such as silicone putty. This enables you to customize bath bombs to reflect the aesthetic preferences of your brand or individual customers.

The Curing And Drying Procedure

1. In contrast to oven drying, bath bombs necessitate appropriate drying and curing processes to preserve their form and efficacy. Although air drying is the prevailing technique, in humid climates it is possible to expedite the process by employing a low-temperature oven.

2. Drying Time: The drying time may differ based on variables such as temperature, volume, and the components employed. In general, bath bubbles require a minimum of twenty-four to forty-eight hours to dry completely before they can be packaged.

3. Touch testing should be performed to ensure that the bath bubbles have completely desiccated and cured. They are desiccated and robust to the touch, devoid of any tender areas; therefore, they are suitable for packaging.

4. While undergoing curing, dry bath bombs in a cold, dry location that is shielded from direct sunlight and moisture. This inhibits their ability to absorb moisture from the surrounding air, which could result in expansion or a loss of their fizziness.

Consignment And Presentation

1. Brand Identity: Construct a unified brand identity that mirrors the distinctive attributes of your bath bombs. This involves selecting colors, materials, and designs for packaging that effectively appeal to the intended consumer base.

2. It is imperative to appropriately label bath bubbles by including critical information such as ingredients, instructions for use, and cautionary statements. This practice fosters customer confidence and guarantees adherence to regulatory requirements.

3. To enhance the visual allure of your bath bombs, contemplate inventive packaging alternatives. For instance, eco-friendly cases, organza bags, or mason vessels could be considered. Incorporating embellishments

such as ribbons or decals can enhance the overall quality of the presentation.

4. Sample sizes and gift sets have the potential to appeal to customers seeking to sample a diverse range of bath salts or fragrances. Furthermore, these items serve as excellent gift choices, particularly on holidays and special events.

5. Branding Materials: To reinforce brand recognition and encourage repeat purchases, incorporate branding materials into your packaging, such as business cards, thank-you notes, or promotional fliers.

Promotion Of Your Bath Bombs

1. Online Presence: Cultivate a robust digital footprint using a specialized website or by utilizing social media platforms. Present compelling content and high-quality images

that highlight your bath salts and the history of your brand.

2. To increase the visibility of your website and online listings in search engine results, optimize them with pertinent keywords. This assists prospective clients in locating your products when conducting an online search for bath bubbles.

3. Develop entertaining and educational content concerning bath bombs, hygiene, and self-care regimens for content marketing. This may consist of user-generated content, blog posts, or instructional videos that feature your products.

4. Collaborations and Partnerships: Expand brand exposure and reach new audiences by collaborating with local businesses, bloggers, or influencers. In return for them endorsing your bath bombs to their followers, extend

exclusive discounts or complimentary samples.

5. Customer Testimonials and Reviews: Motivate contented clientele to provide reviews and testimonials about their encounters with your bath bombs. Positive feedback aids in attracting new customers by fostering confidence and credibility.

Online Sales

1. Select a dependable electronic commerce platform to distribute your bath bombs on the internet. Provide intuitive interfaces and customizable functionalities that efficiently exhibit your products.

2. Produce persuasive product descriptions that emphasize the essential qualities, advantages, and fragrance profiles of your bath bombs. Motivate customers to purchase

by employing descriptive language and vivid narratives.

3. Invest in photography of superior quality to present your bath bubbles in the most favorable manner possible. Purchase decisions can be significantly influenced by colors, textures, and packaging that are captured in images that are well-lit and crystal clear.

4. Customer Service: Deliver exceptional customer service through timely response to inquiries, resolution of concerns, and expedient order processing. Recurring sales and positive consumer interactions have the potential to generate word-of-mouth recommendations.

5. Transportation and Fulfillment: Provide expedient and dependable transportation alternatives to guarantee the punctual

distribution of your bath bombs. Invest in durable packaging materials to safeguard your products while in transit and ensure that your customers have a smooth unboxing experience.

Novices in the burgeoning beauty and self-care sector can establish a prosperous enterprise, magnetize clientele, and manufacture high-quality bath bombs by concentrating on the aforementioned facets of production and distribution.

CHAPTER THREE

Local Markets And Events For Sales

Bath bomb sales at local events and markets can be an excellent way to launch a business and increase its visibility. The following describes one possible approach to this:

1. Investigate Community Events: Seek out nearby craft festivals, farmers' markets, or gatherings at which you can establish a stall. Investigate the organization's vendor requirements, schedule, and costs.

2. Invest in a professional and aesthetically pleasing display for your bath bubbles. To attract consumers, consider utilizing colorful signage, samples, and evaluators.

3. Provide Diversification: Assemble a substantial selection of bath bombs encompassing various sizes, shapes,

fragrances, and appearances to attract a more extensive audience.

4. Maintain a proactive stance towards interacting with prospective consumers. Provide details regarding your products' composition, benefits, and constituents. Provide demonstrations whenever feasible.

5. Acquire Feedback: Leverage this occasion to solicit direct feedback from clientele. Gain insight into the benefits and drawbacks of your products to enhance and customize your offerings.

6. Distribute business cards or fliers to promote your brand. Spectacle discounts or promotions should be considered for consumers who visit your exhibit.

Managing Difficulties

There are obstacles to launching any business and producing and distributing soap bubbles is no different. Listed below are frequent obstacles and strategies for overcoming them:

1. Sourcing of Ingredients: Guarantee a steady provision of high-quality ingredients. Develop solid rapport with suppliers to prevent shortages.

2. Distinguish your products from the competition by providing distinctive fragrances, designs, or packaging. Concentrate on customer service and quality.

3. It is imperative to be cognizant of the local regulations that govern cosmetics and hygiene products. Ensure adherence to safety and labeling regulations.

4. Seasonal demand can be effectively managed through the implementation of a diversified product range. To leverage current trends, provide bath salts with a seasonal or themed theme.

5. Optimize your production process as demand increases to scale production. To increase efficiency, consider outsourcing specific duties or investing in equipment.

6. Customers should be informed about the advantages of bath salts and the distinguishing features of your product. Respond to frequent misunderstandings or concerns.

Expansion Of The Business

To expand your bath explosion enterprise, you must make strategic investments and plans. Specify the following to expand:

1. Expand Production Capacity: To accommodate rising demand, consider investing in larger equipment or outsourcing production.

2. Diversify Distribution Channels: Consider venturing into the online marketplace via your website or prominent e-commerce platforms. Establish collaborations with boutiques and retailers to expand your reach.

3. Expand the range of products available to consumers by introducing complementary items, including bath salts, body treatments, and hygiene sets (product diversification).

4. Develop Brand Recognition: Allocate resources towards marketing initiatives such as influencer collaborations, social media advertising, and participation in major trade shows.

5. Optimize Operations: Establish streamlined inventory management and order fulfillment procedures to effectively manage increased volumes.

6. Maintain a financial ledger by monitoring your revenues, expenses, and profits. To foster expansion, strategically reinvest in your company.

Implement Safety Precautions

Priority number one in the production and sale of bath explosives is safety. Observe the following precautions:

1. Ingredient Quality: Only utilize skin-safe, high-quality ingredients; refrain from employing abrasive compounds.

2. Observe proper manufacturing procedures by keeping the work area tidy and organized.

Observe hygienic procedures to avert contamination.

3. Packaging and Labeling: Ensure that your products are appropriately labeled with the following information: ingredients, usage instructions, and any applicable warnings. Use packaging that is resistant to children when storing specific products.

4. Aware of Common Allergens: Ensure that these allergens are disclosed plainly on your products.

5. Conduct stability and safety tests to guarantee that your products are fit for human consumption.

6. Maintain comprehensive documentation about your formulations, manufacturing procedures, and safety evaluations.

Comprehending The Target Market

A comprehensive understanding of one's target market is critical for achieving success. Please take into account the following procedures:

1. As part of your market research, determine who purchases bath bubbles. Comprehend consumer preferences, demographics, and purchasing patterns.

2. Consumer Personas: By your investigation, develop consumer profiles. Consider aspects such as spending tendencies, age, gender, and way of life.

3. Benefits and Pain Points: Recognize the reasons why clients utilize bath explosives. Emphasize advantages including those related to relaxation, hygiene, and aromatherapy.

4. Consideration should be given to consumer reviews and feedback. By analyzing reviews and testimonials, you can determine what aspects of your audience resonate with them.

5. Gain insights by interacting with consumers via social media, surveys, or events.

6. Adapt and Pivot: Recognize market trends and customer feedback to modify your offerings and maintain competitiveness.

You will be well on your way to establishing a prosperous bath bomb enterprise by attaining proficiency in the following concepts: selling at local markets, surmounting obstacles, expanding operations, guaranteeing safety, and comprehending your target market.

38

CHAPTER FOUR

Developing Spectacular Bath Bomb Designs

Producing and marketing bath salts can prove to be a lucrative enterprise, particularly for individuals who are new to the world of handcrafted cosmetics. There is much to consider, including the creation of one-of-a-kind designs, the resolution of common problems, pricing strategies, the establishment of a workspace, and product and inventory management. Let us thoroughly examine each of these concepts:

1. Components and Formulation: To commence, acquire a fundamental comprehension of the constituents that comprise a bath bomb, which is customarily baking soda, citric acid, Epsom salts, essential oils, and coloring agents. Explore

diverse amalgamations to attain an assortment of odors, hues, and textures.

2. Molds and Forms: To replicate a variety of sizes and shapes, purchase an assortment of molds. The assortment may encompass conventional spherical molds as well as more elaborate creations such as animals, florals, or geometric figures. Frequently, silicone molds are favored due to their adaptability and simplicity of use.

3. Enhance ingenuity through the utilization of embods and layering diverse hues, or incorporate ornamental components such as dehydrated flowers, botanicals, or biodegradable glitter. This can increase the perceived value of your bath bubbles by adding visual appeal.

4. Customization and Personalization: One potential avenue for expanding your customer

base is by providing customizable offerings, including bath bombs adorned with concealed surprises such as miniature toys or messages, monogrammed initials, and thematic designs intended for holidays or special occasions.

5. For inspiration and guidance, remain informed about the latest developments in bath and body products, in addition to seasonal motifs. You can generate distinctive and marketable designs by deriving inspiration from natural phenomena, popular culture, or even culinary trends.

Troubleshooting Frequent Problems

1. Cracking or Fizzing: Moisture exposure or insufficient binding agents may be the cause of premature cracking or fizzing in your bath bubbles. Ensure that the ingredients have been thoroughly combined and that the

mixture has been firmly compacted into the molds. Additionally, hermetic storage containers can aid in preventing the absorption of moisture.

2. Color Bleeding: The presence of color bleeding or muddled colors could potentially be attributed to the utilization of water-based colorants or the excessive addition of moisture during the mixing procedure. It is advisable to contemplate the use of oil-based colorants or decrease the liquid content of the recipe.

3. If the fragrance of your bath bombs fades away too soon, this may be the result of using fragrance oils of inferior quality or not adding enough. Ensure that the skin-safe, high-quality fragrance oils are distributed uniformly throughout the mixture.

4. Texture Challenges: To achieve bath bombs that are excessively fuzzy or brittle, the proportions of the ingredients may be off, or the drying time may be insufficient. After adjusting the formulation to attain the intended consistency, permit the bath bombs to completely dry before packaging.

Cost Of Your Bath Bombs

1. The base cost of each bath bomb is determined by calculating the costs of ingredients, packaging, labor, and administrative expenses. For precise pricing, both variable and fixed costs must be accounted for.

2. Conduct market research on comparable bath bomb prices in your target market to determine how much consumers are willing to pay. When establishing your prices, consider

the distinctiveness of your designs and the superior quality of your ingredients.

3. Value Proposition: Emphasize the distinctive attributes of your bath bombs, including their organic composition, adaptable configurations, or exclusive aesthetics, to convey their worth to customers. Highlighting the advantages they provide, including relaxation, hygiene benefits, and aromatherapy.

4. Establish a profit margin that facilitates the long-term viability and expansion of your enterprise. Aim to achieve a balance between consumer affordability and business profitability.

5. Wholesale and Retail Pricing: To attract resellers and retailers, consider offering wholesale pricing on bulk orders. After volume discounts have been accounted for,

ensure that your wholesale prices still permit a fair profit margin.

Establishing A Workspace

1. Hygiene and Safety: To uphold product quality and safety standards, it is imperative to maintain a clean and sanitized workspace. When handling constituents, adhere to good manufacturing practices (GMP) and utilize the proper personal protective equipment (PPE).

2. Invest in bath bomb-making equipment and instruments of superior quality, including measuring utensils, and combining containers, scales, and molds. Effectively arrange your work area to optimize the workflow of your production.

3. Storage and Organization: To prevent contamination and deterioration, store ingredients and supplies in labeled containers. Maintain an orderly and clutter-

free workspace to reduce errors and increase productivity.

4. Ventilation: It is crucial to maintain sufficient ventilation in one's work area, particularly when handling volatile substances such as fragrances. This facilitates the elimination of pollutants and preserves a pleasant working environment.

5. It is imperative to acquaint oneself with the local regulations and prerequisites that govern the production and distribution of bath and body products. This may entail the acquisition of necessary permits, adherence to labeling regulations, and compliance with safety standards.

CHAPTER FIVE

Management Of Inventory And Records

1. Inventory Management: Maintain a record of the quantities of ingredients, packaging materials, and finished products in your inventory. Incorporate a systematic approach, such as a spreadsheet or inventory management software, to oversee stock levels and reorder necessary supplies.

2. Maintain comprehensive batch records for every production run, encompassing pertinent information such as quantities and formulations of ingredients, dates of production, and pertinent notes or observations. This contributes to the traceability and consistency of your products.

3. It is imperative to maintain comprehensive records of sales transactions and expenses,

encompassing expenditures related to ingredients, packaging, marketing, and administration. This data is crucial for making informed decisions and evaluating the financial performance of your organization.

4. Quality Control: To ensure the quality and consistency of your bath bubbles, implement quality control measures. Ensure that finalized products are routinely inspected for defects or deviations from quality standards, and implement any necessary corrective measures.

5. Consumer Feedback: Obtain insights regarding consumer preferences, levels of satisfaction, and any encountered issues by soliciting customer feedback. Utilize this feedback to enhance your products and the consumer experience continuously.

Beginner bath bomb makers can establish a solid groundwork for success by concentrating on the following fundamental principles: developing distinctive designs, resolving frequent problems, setting competitive prices for their products, organizing a productive work environment, and implementing reliable record-keeping and inventory management systems.

Establishing Brand Identity

It is vital to establish a brand identity when manufacturing and distributing bath bubbles for novices. It goes beyond selecting colors and designing a logo; it involves articulating the values and intended perception of your brand among customers. Consider the following approach:

1. Define your values: Which principles do you wish to be embodied by your brand?

Specify what distinguishes your brand, be it luxury, sustainability, or enjoyment.

2. Establish a Distinct Visual Identity: Construct a logo, select colors, and generate visual components that embody the character of your brand. Ensure that these components are uniform throughout your online presence, packaging, and marketing materials.

3. Describe Your Brand: Describe the history of your brand. Just why did you begin producing bath bombs? What motivates you to create? Authentic storytelling fosters a more profound connection between your brand and your customers.

4. Establishing a Uniform Brand Voice: Cultivate a unified brand voice that seamlessly transitions between lighthearted, informative, and opulent tones. Incorporate

this tone into your customer interactions, product descriptions, and social media posts.

5. Construct a Community: Foster interaction with your clientele via email newsletters, social media platforms, and even physical gatherings. Promoting the exchange of personal experiences regarding your products will cultivate a communal atmosphere surrounding your brand.

6. Ensuring Consistency and Quality: Promptly provide products of superior quality. This strengthens the bond between you and your customers and the reputation of your brand.

7. Adapt and Evolve: Be receptive to the modification of your brand identity as your company expands. It is imperative to maintain steadfastness in one's fundamental principles while remaining flexible in

response to evolving market dynamics or consumer inclinations.

Cooperating With Additional Artisans

Partnering with other artisans can serve as an advantageous strategy to broaden one's assortment of products and enter untapped markets. Here's how to accomplish it efficiently:

1. Determine Complementary Artisans: Seek out craftspeople whose wares harmonize with your own. You could, for instance, collaborate with a manufacturer of handcrafted candles, detergents, or hygiene products.

2. Form Mutually Beneficial Partnerships: Propose to prospective collaborators a well-defined alliance that delineates how the collaboration would yield advantages for all

involved. This may involve co-hosted events, cross-promotion, or joint product bundles.

3. Maintain Clear Communication: To prevent misunderstandings, define each party's roles and responsibilities in detail from the outset. Consistent communication is essential for the seamless operation of the collaboration.

4. Quality Control: Ensure that your collaborators' products conform to your quality requirements. This may entail the provision of guidelines or instructions to guarantee uniformity.

5. Commemorate the Collaboration: Upon the launch of the collaboration, commemorate it through your official website and social media platforms. By doing so, you not only enhance the visibility of the partnership but also fortify your brand's reputation as a cooperative and community-focused enterprise.

6. Evaluate and Gain Insights: Conduct a post-collaboration assessment of its efficacy. What was successful? What might be altered for the future? Utilize this feedback to refine your approach and guide future collaborations.

Growing Your Product Portfolio

In addition to increasing sales, expanding your product line can help you attract new consumers. The following are several stages to contemplate:

1. Market Research: To begin, conduct market research to identify potential market gaps and emerging trends that may present opportunities for financial gain. Consider conducting a customer satisfaction survey to determine which products your current clientele would be most interested in.

2. Start Small: Avoid introducing an excessive number of new

products simultaneously. Before expanding further, begin with one or two new products and gauge consumer interest and feedback.

3. Customer feedback should be duly considered, and suggestions put forth by customers should be incorporated into the product development process. This practice not only enhances the likelihood of favorable reception for your new products but also cultivates customer loyalty.

4. Ensuring Brand Cohesion: Although providing a diverse range of products is essential, ensure that they are consistent with the established brand identity and core values. This contributes to the preservation of brand cohesion and serves to avert consumer confusion.

5. Quality Control: Guarantee that the quality of any newly introduced products is

equivalent to that of your current offerings. This safeguards the reputation of your brand and guarantees customer contentment.

6. After your new products have been developed and are prepared for release, allocate sufficient time and energy towards promoting them via your website, social media platforms, and email newsletters. Consider generating interest by providing exclusive discounts or promotions.

7. Assess Performance: Following the introduction of your novel products, diligently monitor their performance. It is advisable to closely monitor sales figures, consumer feedback, and any other pertinent metrics. Apply the acquired data to enhance your future product offerings and marketing strategies.

CHAPTER SIX

Customer Feedback And Satisfaction

Customer contentment and feedback are critical components in establishing a prosperous bath explosion enterprise. You can ensure that you are meeting the needs of your customers as follows:

1. Promote Feedback: Facilitate the provision of feedback by consumers regarding their experiences with your products. This may be accomplished via online reviews, surveys, or order-accompanying feedback forms.

2. Actively Listen: Invest effort in attentively hearing the perspectives of your consumers, including both positive and constructive criticism. Utilize this feedback to identify enhancement areas and implement the required modifications.

3. Provide Prompt and Professional Responses: To effectively address customer inquiries or feedback, ensure that your responses are timely and conducted professionally. This demonstrates that you are committed to delivering exceptional customer service and value their input.

4. Respond Proactively to Issues: If a consumer encounters a negative experience, adopt a proactive stance to resolve the matter to their complete satisfaction. This may entail extending a replacement product, reimbursement, or other forms of benevolent gestures.

5. Commemorate Positive Feedback: Express gratitude in a public manner and disseminate the feedback of consumers who provide favorable testimonials or reviews on your website and social media platforms.

This not only serves as an expression of gratitude for their assistance but also fosters confidence among prospective clients.

6. Leverage Feedback for Improvement: Opt for ongoing analysis of customer feedback to discern recurring issues or patterns. Incorporate this data into your product development, service provision, and overall customer experience enhancement strategies.

7. Assess Customer Satisfaction: Establish mechanisms to gauge customer satisfaction, such as customer satisfaction ratings or Net Promoter Score (NPS) surveys. Track your performance over time and identify areas for development using these metrics.

Regulatory And Legal Factors To Consider

It is crucial for any enterprise, including one that manufactures and distributes bath bubbles, to traverse the legal and regulatory terrain. Here are several crucial factors to bear in mind:

1. It is imperative to verify that the bath bubbles in question adhere to all pertinent safety regulations about the product's composition, labeling, and packaging. If necessary, investigate the regulations in your jurisdiction and consult an attorney.

2. Safeguard the intellectual property of your brand through the registration of trademarks that include your brand name, logo, and any other distinguishing characteristics. Use copyrighted materials with caution when

creating marketing materials or product designs.

3. Business Registration: Obtain any licenses or permits required to operate legally in your jurisdiction and register your company. Depending on your location, this may involve a business license, sales tax permit, or health department permit.

4. Tax Compliance: Conscious of your sales tax, income tax, and any other pertinent taxes, as a business proprietor, you must be aware of your tax obligations. Income and expense documents should be kept accurate to facilitate tax reporting and compliance.

5. Contractual Agreements: It is imperative to establish unambiguous contractual agreements with other artisans or suppliers to delineate the respective rights and obligations of each party involved in any

collaborative endeavor. This safeguards your interests and aids in preventing misunderstandings.

6. Adherence to pertinent data protection legislation, including the General Data Protection Regulation (GDPR) in the European Union, is imperative when gathering personal information from consumers, be it via email newsletters or online sales.

7. It is crucial for businesses to adhere to environmental regulations, particularly those that pertain to the use of packaging materials or ingredients that may potentially affect the environment.

Encourage the implementation of sustainable practices to reduce one's ecological impact.

Sustainability Methods Of Action

In addition to benefiting the environment, incorporating sustainable practices into your bath bomb enterprise may also appeal to environmentally conscious customers. Incorporate sustainability into your business in the following ways:

1. Sustainable Ingredients: Whenever possible, select ingredients for your bath bombs that are natural, biodegradable, and sourced sustainably. Avoid environmentally hazardous or unsustainably sourced ingredients, including palm oil and microplastics.

2. Choose packaging that is both eco-friendly and minimal when presenting your products. This could include packaging designs that minimize waste and recycled or biodegradable materials.

3. It is advisable to contemplate the provision of packaging alternatives that are reusable or refillable in nature for your bath bombs. Customers can reduce pollution by refilling their containers rather than constantly purchasing new ones.

4. Energy-Efficient Production: Construct your manufacturing process with energy-efficient practices in mind, including the utilization of energy-efficient equipment and the optimization of your production schedule to reduce energy usage.

5. Waste Reduction: Throughout the production process, minimize waste by optimizing constituent usage, recycling or repurposing refuse materials, and, whenever practicable, implementing waste reduction strategies.

6. Participate in sustainability initiatives within your community, including beach cleanups, tree-planting events, and collaborations with environmental organizations. Engaging in such actions not only showcases one's dedication to sustainability but also cultivates positive sentiment and enhances the standing of the brand.

7. Maintaining Transparency in Communication: Ensure that your consumers are aware of the environmental impact of your products and your sustainability initiatives. Please furnish details about your product's sourcing procedures, packaging components, and any applicable certifications or eco-labels.

You can reduce the environmental impact of your bath bomb business, attract environmentally conscious customers, and make a positive contribution to a more sustainable future by incorporating these sustainable practices.

Conclusion

As a conclusion, it can be both thrilling and lucrative for a novice to enter the realm of bath bomb manufacturing and distribution. This expedition teaches one not only the craftsmanship involved in producing aesthetically pleasing bath bombs but also the complexities associated with managing a small enterprise.

Novices must begin by conducting extensive research and conducting experiments to comprehend the ingredients, processes, and market demand. Obtaining knowledge from tutorials, online courses, or bath bomb maker communities can offer invaluable assistance and support.

In an increasingly competitive market, it is critical to prioritize constituent quality, fragrance combinations, and aesthetic allure as one advance. Furthermore, the establishment of an online presence via e-commerce websites or social media platforms can substantially increase market penetration and clientele.

Notwithstanding the fervor, it is critical to effectively manage obstacles including scalability, pricing strategies, and regulatory compliance. Constant education, flexibility, and fervor for crafting enjoyable bathing encounters are critical factors in maintaining and expanding a bath bomb enterprise.

In essence, the process of producing and vending bath bombs as an entry-level practitioner encompasses more than mere financial gain; it also cultivates ingenuity, establishes connections with clientele, and provides the satisfaction derived from constructing a unique item for personal hygiene regimens.

THE END

Made in United States
Troutdale, OR
06/20/2024